This composition notebook belongs to

Made in the USA
Monee, IL
04 October 2021

79312129R00059